T0115206

Maintain Your High

63 Days To
A Better
YOU!

DR. RACHEL FORD STEPHENS

authorHOUSE®

AuthorHouse™
1663 Liberty Drive
Bloomington, IN 47403
www.authorhouse.com
Phone: 833-262-8899

Published by AuthorHouse 04/05/2021

ISBN: 978-1-6655-0913-8 (sc)
ISBN: 978-1-6655-0912-1 (e)

Print information available on the last page.

Scripture quotations marked KJV are from the Holy Bible, King James Version (Authorized Version). First published in 1611. Quoted from the KJV Classic Reference Bible, Copyright © 1983 by The Zondervan Corporation.

This book is printed on acid-free paper.

Dedication

The saying, "the only thing that wants a change is a baby", implies that not many people welcome a change. With that in mind, this journal is dedicated to those who, like the baby, have become "uncomfortable" with the state they are in and are ready for a change.

main•tain – /manˡ tan/

- Cause or enable to continue.
- Keep at the same level or rate.
- Keep in good condition or in working order by checking or repairing it regularly.

your – /yôr/

- Belonging to or associated with the person or people that the speaker is addressing.

high – /hi/

- Great, or greater than normal, in quantity, size, or intensity.

Contents

Introduction

Watch your thoughts for they become words,
Watch your words for they become actions,
Watch your actions, for they become habits,
Watch your habits, for they become your character,
Watch your character for it becomes your destiny.

- Ralph Waldo Emerson

This quote by Emerson suggests your thoughts are the beginning/the genesis of your destiny and one should guard them with caution for they have a profound impact on the direction of one's life journey. There are levels of change that you go through as you walk into your destiny and each should be guarded with the same prudence and energy that was given to your first thought. What you think about yourself, life conditions, and how you perceive others and their involvement in your life are important to your thought process. Romans 12: 2 says, *"And be not conformed to this world: but be ye transformed by the renewing of your mind, that ye may prove what is that good, and acceptable, and perfect, will of God."* Your mind…your new thoughts are the beginning of your change/transformation that inevitably determines your destiny.

This journal is to assist and encourage you in the transformation of your life. It is about changing something(s)/

thought(s) in your life that you think is slowing you down or preventing you from becoming your personal best. It is also to help in *maintaining* a consistent level of thought(s), perseverance, and energy until that goal(s) has been achieved.

You may be aware that your life is changing, but you are not evolving in a way that make you feel as though you are moving in the direction of your destiny. You may have thought that your life's journey would surely change when you received that chosen degree, the job/location, the husband/wife, home, or became an empty nester. After achieving all these milestones, you feel tethered to a pilgrimage of a nomadic journey. In spite of everything, your destiny seems to be just as much beyond your reach as it did years ago. What is it that seems to keep you stuck in a nomadic or cyclic mode? Could it be something you are doing or have done that keeps you here? Could it be the very thoughts that you are thinking holding you back?

Read the following "Preparation for the Journey" before you begin journaling. This will aid in understanding the process of journaling.

Preparation for the Journey

1. ***Write a brief autobiography.*** Have you ever taken the time to write about your personal life's journey? Take the time to do so now. Begin this journey with *your story.* You may begin with your born day, an outstanding event, or any point in your life. As you are writing, feel free to stop along the way and highlight events in your life; those things that you feel changed you – the good, the bad, and the ugly.

Socrates said, "The unexamined life is not worth living for a human being." This autobiography will help examine things you practiced/accepted and reveal some things that may have found a hiding place in your subconscious. In doing so, it may also give you a view/perception of yourself that you have not seen. Most importantly, it will help you assess and make appropriate/necessary adjustments about your thoughts or behaviors during these 63 days.

2. ***Weekly encouragement,*** along with a word for the week, is given to add fuel to your day/week. As you go through this process, feel free to reread or revisit any section that you find beneficial. Remember, it is all about maintaining a high level of energy.

WHAT TO DO – Your daily routine

3. *My Dream/My Thoughts.* In your distinctively designed brain, you have the ability to bring every thought into captivity. You have 30 to 60 thousand thoughts or more each day.[1] You choose which thoughts you want to hold onto and which thoughts you allow to pass through your brain. This journal is about choosing positive thoughts that will give you peace, allow you to walk in the things of God, and not hinder you from becoming the best YOU.

   Second Corinthians says, *"Casting down imaginations, and every high thing that exalteth itself against the knowledge of God, and bringing into captivity every thought to the obedience of Christ;"*

   Write down a more constructive and optimistic version of the thoughts that you are seeking to change. Write it daily.

4. *Daydream!!!* Daydreaming is important. It helps to sell yourself daily on your dream. Research has shown that thinking positive about 6 to 16 minutes at the beginning of your day will greatly aid in it being pleasant and successful.[2] This will help maintain your focus and discipline your mind from dwelling on things that are unproductive.

Write a brief summary of your daydream and record the time.

5. ***Letting Go!*** Let go of any negative thought; the one you chose to pass through your brain and would have normally held residence. As they come, write it down immediately and cross through it as a reminder that you have allowed its passage. Although the space is provided, you may choose not to make a journal entry.

6. ***Invest in yourself.*** Speak over and incite yourself with a daily positive note. Bathing your mind in positive thinking can do wonders in your pursuit of change. Maintaining a level of excitement can come from within. Be grateful!

My Autobiography

_____
_____
_____
_____
_____
_____
_____
_____
_____
_____
_____
_____
_____
_____
_____
_____
_____
_____
_____
_____
_____
_____
_____
_____
_____
_____

After writing my autobiography and analyzing my life, I have concluded that the thought/action I want to change is:

_____

_____

_____

_____

_____

_____

_____

_____

_____

_____

_____

_____

_____

With this change, I will be able to:

_____

_____

_____

_____

_____

_____

_____

_____

_____

Week One

...maintain...

WEEK ONE: *MAINTAIN YOUR HIGH*

The week of ___/___/___ through ___/___/___

Your Weekly Motivation

"These things I have spoken unto you, that in me ye might have peace. In the world ye shall have tribulation: but be of good cheer; I have overcome the world."

John 16: 33

Word for the week – *Maintain*

(Keep at the same level or rate)

Now that you have decided what thought you want to change, there is or should be a high level of excitement and anticipation about your journey. This excitement should be maintained as much as possible throughout the week.

Day 1 – 4 will be fairly easy, because you are in high expectation of a great outcome. Your brain has just released some important chemicals that are primarily responsible for your high level of excitement. They are:

Serotonin: a neurotransmitter that contributes to feelings of well-being and happiness.

Dopamine: a neurotransmitter that plays a major role in the motivational component of reward-motivated behavior.[3] Unfortunately, the levels of these neurotransmitters are greatly reduced after the first 4 days. This is when you will begin to feel a return of apathy. Therefore, it becomes increasingly vital; you must maintain your high levels of neurotransmitters. Recognize it and promptly stimulate your brain to release serotonin and dopamine. The anticipation of a great outcome of your journey will help maintain a high level of dopamine and serotonin. An attitude of gratefulness and thanksgiving will go a long way in the success of this journey. These 63 days are about making a permanent change through maintaining your expectation as you maintain your high.

Week One – Day One

Day: _____; Date: ____/____/____; Time: _____

Maintain

"Finally, brethren, whatsoever things are true, whatsoever things are honest, whatsoever things are just, whatsoever things are pure, whatsoever things are lovely, whatsoever things are of good report; if there be any virtue, and if there be any praise, think on these things."

Philippians 4: 8

My thought/ My Daydream

_____

_____

_____

_____

_____

_____

Today I daydreamed for _____ minutes.

A thought that I allowed to pass through my brain. (*Remember to cross through it.*)

_____

_____

_____

_____

_____

_____

_____

I spoke / invested this into myself today.

_____

_____

_____

_____

_____

_____

_____

_____

_____

_____

_____

_____

_____

_____

_____

_____

Week One – Day Two

Day: _____; Date: ____/____/____; Time: _____

Maintain

"Hold fast the form of sound words, which thou hast heard of me, in faith and love which is in Christ Jesus."

2 Timothy 1: 13

My thought/ My Daydream

_____

_____

_____

_____

_____

_____

Today I daydreamed for _____ minutes.

A thought that I allowed to pass through my brain. (*Remember to cross through it.*)

_____
_____
_____
_____
_____
_____
_____

I spoke / invested this into myself today.

_____
_____
_____
_____
_____
_____
_____
_____
_____
_____
_____
_____
_____
_____
_____
_____

Week One – Day Three

Day: _____; Date: ____/____/____; Time: _____

Maintain

"Then hear thou from the heavens their prayer and their supplication, and maintain their cause."

2 Chronicles 6: 35

My thought/ My Daydream

_____

_____

_____

_____

_____

_____

Today I daydreamed for _____ minutes.

A thought that I allowed to pass through my brain. (*Remember to cross through it.*)

_____

_____

_____

_____

_____

_____

_____

I spoke / invested this into myself today.

_____

_____

_____

_____

_____

_____

_____

_____

_____

_____

_____

_____

_____

_____

_____

_____

Week One – Day Four

Day: _____; Date: _____/_____/_____; Time: _____

Maintain

"This is a faithful saying, and these things I will that thou affirm constantly, that they which have believed in God might be careful to maintain good works. These things are good and profitable unto men."

Titus 3: 8

My thought/ My Daydream

_____

_____

_____

_____

_____

_____

Today I daydreamed for _____ minutes.

A thought that I allowed to pass through my brain. (*Remember to cross through it.*)

_____

_____

_____

_____

_____

_____

I spoke / invested this into myself today.

_____

_____

_____

_____

_____

_____

_____

_____

_____

_____

_____

_____

_____

_____

Week One – Day Five

Day: _____; Date: ____/____/____; Time: _____

Maintain

"And let ours also learn to maintain good works for necessary uses, that they be not unfruitful."

Titus 3: 14

My thought/ My Daydream

_____

_____

_____

_____

_____

_____

Today I daydreamed for _____ **minutes.**

A thought that I allowed to pass through my brain. (*Remember to cross through it.*)

_____

_____

_____

_____

_____

_____

_____

I spoke / invested this into myself today.

_____

_____

_____

_____

_____

_____

_____

_____

_____

_____

_____

_____

_____

_____

_____

_____

_____

Week One – Day Six

Day: _____; Date: ____/____/____; Time: _____

Maintain

*"For as the heavens are higher than the
earth, so are my ways higher than your ways,
and my thoughts than your thoughts."*

Isaiah 55: 9

My thought/ My Daydream

_____

_____

_____

_____

_____

_____

Today I daydreamed for _____ minutes.

A thought that I allowed to pass through my brain. (*Remember to cross through it.*)

_____

_____

_____

_____

_____

_____

_____

I spoke / invested this into myself today.

_____

_____

_____

_____

_____

_____

_____

_____

_____

_____

_____

_____

_____

_____

_____

_____

_____

Week One – Day Seven

Day: _____ ; Date: ____/____/____ ; Time: _____

Maintain

"Now unto him that is able to do exceeding
abundantly above all that we ask or think,
according to the power that worketh in us, ..."

Ephesians 3: 20

My thought/ My Daydream

_____

_____

_____

_____

_____

_____

Today I daydreamed for _____ minutes.

A thought that I allowed to pass through my brain. (*Remember to cross through it.*)

_____

_____

_____

_____

_____

_____

I spoke / invested this into myself today.

_____

_____

_____

_____

_____

_____

_____

_____

_____

_____

_____

_____

_____

_____

_____

_____

Week Two

WEEK TWO: *PURSUE*

The week of ___/___/___ through ___/___/___

Your Weekly Motivation

*"Now faith is the substance of things hoped
for, the evidence of things not seen."*

Hebrews 11: 1

Word for the week —*Pursue*

(To push yourself to do something until you have attained it.)

Sometimes a person may hold onto defeating words, negative thoughts, and/or dream killing actions, because they are unable to see a profitable end. But God said, *"I know the thoughts that I think toward you, saith the LORD, thoughts of peace, and not of evil, to give an expected end."*

A few years ago, I was going through a period of discouragement and could not see any productivity in my life. I was frustrated and almost at a point of relinquishing any hope of better. One night, as sleep could not find a place of rest, I cried out to God, "Lord there has to be more!!!" I have found when the right question has been asked with heartfelt sincerity, there is an answer. And He said, "Pursue." Again I asked, not sure of if He was truly responding, "What Lord?" He said it again, "Pursue." All through the night, I heard a resounding "Pursue." At daybreak, upon wakening, I heard, "Pursue." I asked, "What do you mean

LORD?" He took me to Hebrews 11: 1, *"Now faith is the substance of things hoped for, the evidence of things not seen."*

In this verse, John Calvin describes the word *"substance"* as *"to apprehend"*. Apprehend is synonymous with the words catch, capture, arrest, and seize. If you were to replace substance in the verse with the word apprehend, that would mean your faith is pursuing and capturing what it is that you are hoping for, just as a police apprehends a suspect. Your faith is evidence; the proof of what you are hoping for, what you are pursuing will come to past.

Note the "Now" at the beginning of the verse. Now is always in the present tense; the present moment, right now. Your faith is in a constant state of pursuance.

I questioned God as to where was faith holding the things I was hoping for. He then took me to Psalm 37: 33, *"The steps of a good man are ordered by the Lord..."* At this point, I need you to visualize a set of steps and you are at the bottom looking up with an aspiration to reach the top. You have a desire, a hope and faith in God to bring it to fruition. Now faith apprehends the hope and places it on the bottom step. Each subsequent step is holding a new hope. As you move from faith to faith, step to step, and as you live a life of faith, you receive the things that you hoped for. Imagine, as you step up onto each step, you pick up the things you were hoping for. A higher hope requires a stronger determination of faith. Keep in mind that faith without works is dead. The works are in your persistent pursuit.

As you are journaling each day, have faith that what you are working to change will change. Maintain your high translates into your "**now renewed or countinued faith**" in your pursuit.

Week Two – Day Eight

Day: _____; Date: ____/____/____; Time: _____

Pursue

"My brethren, count it all joy when ye fall into divers temptation; Knowing this, that the trying of your faith worketh patience. But let patience have her perfect and entire, wanting nothing."

James 1: 2-4

My thought/ My Daydream

_____

_____

_____

_____

_____

_____

Today I daydreamed for _____ minutes.

A thought that I allowed to pass through my brain. (*Remember to cross through it.*)

_____
_____
_____
_____
_____
_____
_____

I spoke / invested this into myself today.

_____
_____
_____
_____
_____
_____
_____
_____
_____
_____
_____
_____
_____
_____
_____
_____
_____

Week Two – Day Nine

Day: _____; Date: ____/____/____; Time: _____

Pursue

*"And beside this, giving all diligence, add to your faith
virtue; and to virtue knowledge; And to knowledge
temperance; and to temperance patience; and to
patience godliness; And to godliness brotherly
kindness; and to brotherly kindness charity. For
if these things be in you, and abound, they make
you that ye shall neither be barren nor unfruitful
in the knowledge of our Lord Jesus Christ."*

2 Peter 1: 5-8

My thought/ My Daydream

_____

_____

_____

_____

_____

_____

Today I daydreamed for _____ minutes.

A thought that I allowed to pass through my brain. (*Remember to cross through it.*)

_____

_____

_____

_____

_____

_____

I spoke / invested this into myself today.

_____

_____

_____

_____

_____

_____

_____

_____

_____

_____

_____

_____

_____

_____

_____

Week Two – Day Ten

Day: _____; Date: _____/_____/_____; Time: _____

Pursue

"I know thy works, and charity, and service,
and faith, and thy patience, and thy works;
and the last to be more than the first."

Revelation 2: 19

My thought/ My Daydream

_____

_____

_____

_____

_____

_____

Today I daydreamed for _____ minutes.

A thought that I allowed to pass through my brain. (*Remember to cross through it.*)

_____

_____

_____

_____

_____

_____

I spoke / invested this into myself today.

_____

_____

_____

_____

_____

_____

_____

_____

_____

_____

_____

_____

_____

_____

_____

_____

Week Two – Day Eleven

Day: _____; Date: ____/____/____; Time: _____

Pursue

"Now set your heart and your soul to
seek the LORD your God;..."

1 Chronicles 22: 19

My thought/ My Daydream

_____

_____

_____

_____

_____

_____

Today I daydreamed for _____ minutes.

A thought that I allowed to pass through my brain. (*Remember to cross through it.*)

_____
_____
_____
_____
_____
_____
_____

I spoke / invested this into myself today.

_____
_____
_____
_____
_____
_____
_____
_____
_____
_____
_____
_____
_____
_____
_____
_____
_____

Week Two – Day Twelve

Day: _____; Date: ____/____/____; Time: _____

Pursue

"Even so faith, if it hath not works, is dead, being alone."

James 2: 17

My thought/ My Daydream

_____

_____

_____

_____

_____

_____

Today I daydreamed for _____ minutes.

A thought that I allowed to pass through my brain. (*Remember to cross through it.*)

_____

_____

_____

_____

_____

_____

_____

I spoke / invested this into myself today.

_____

_____

_____

_____

_____

_____

_____

_____

_____

_____

_____

_____

_____

_____

_____

_____

Day: _____; Date: ____/____/____; Time: _____

Pursue

"They profess that they know God; but in works they deny him, being abominable, and disobedient, and unto every good work reprobate."

Titus 1: 16

My thought/ My Daydream

_____

_____

_____

_____

_____

_____

Today I daydreamed for _____ minutes.

A thought that I allowed to pass through my brain. *(Remember to cross through it.)*

_____

_____

_____

_____

_____

_____

I spoke / invested this into myself today.

_____

_____

_____

_____

_____

_____

_____

_____

_____

_____

_____

_____

_____

_____

Week Two – Day Fourteen

Day: _____; Date: _____/_____/_____; Time: _____

Pursue

"Order my steps in thy word: and let not
any iniquity have dominion over me."

Psalm 119: 133

My thought/ My Daydream

_____

_____

_____

_____

_____

_____

Today I daydreamed for _____ minutes.

A thought that I allowed to pass through my brain. (*Remember to cross through it.*)

_____

_____

_____

_____

_____

_____

_____

I spoke / invested this into myself today.

_____

_____

_____

_____

_____

_____

_____

_____

_____

_____

_____

_____

_____

_____

_____

_____

_____

Week Three

WEEK THREE: *WRESTLE FOR YOUR REST*

The week of ___/___/___ through ___/___/___

Your Weekly Motivation

""And Jacob was left alone; and there wrestled a man with him until the breaking of the day.... And he said, Let me go, for the day breaketh. And he said, I will not let thee go, except thou bless me."

Genesis 32: 24, 26

Word for the week – *Wrestle*

(Struggle with a difficulty or problem.)

Blessed quietness, holy quietness,
What assurance in my soul.
On the stormy sea,
Jesus Speaks to me.
And the billows cease to roll.

Maine Payne Ferguson

The chorus of the hymn "Blessed Quietness" declares that there can be rest when Jesus speaks to you. The billows, the troubles in your life are calmed with His voice. There is a place of rest for a weary soul. This place of rest/quietness for the soul can only be found in Jesus.

Rest for the soul cannot be found in the inactivity of the body or retreating to your home after a demanding day. The rest for the soul/spirit has to compete with the amusements and struggles of the world. Amusements (TV, Social Media, etc.) are designed to keep you from thinking about your spirituality. The concerns of the world will steal your joy and your peace. You have to wrestle with the things of the world/billows to gain the rest.

Jacob, in the book of Genesis chapter 32, is returning home. His brother had threatened to kill him after stealing his father's blessing. Many years had passed; he now has family, servants, and cattle. Afraid for the safety of his household, Jacob sent them ahead of him, in two separate groups.

Jacob, being left alone, had an encounter with God. He wrestled for a blessing of his soul. He wanted peace, protection, and probably forgiveness. He hungered for rest from his weariness, for he said, "I won't let go until you bless me." He received his rest and most importantly, he also received a name change indicating a new assignment for his life. The direction of his journey was changed from just being the grandson of Abraham and the son of Isaac to being the father of 12 sons that would become the 12 tribes of Israel. These tribes would give birth to our Savior. Jacob was destined to be Israel, but it was in the wrestle that his path was aligned with destiny.

When you find yourself in a predicament you have to wrestle for your rest and your peace. Wrestle in prayer, wrestle with your praise, and wrestle in the study of the word. Jesus speaks to you in His WORD. The WORD of God is living. They are not just words on paper. That's why you feel a leap on the inside when you hear a rhema word. A new identity, a new revelation of yourself awaits you in the wrestle!!!

Week Three – Day Fifteen

Day: _____; Date: ____/____/____; Time: _____

Wrestle

"He maketh wars to cease unto the end of the earth;
He breaketh the bow, and cutteth the spear in sunder;
He burneth the chariots in the fire. Be still, and
know that I am God: I will be exalted among the
nations, I will be exalted in the earth. Jehovah of
hosts is with us; The God of Jacob is our refuge."

Psalm 46: 9-11

My thought/ My Daydream

_____

_____

_____

_____

_____

_____

Today I daydreamed for _____ minutes.

A thought that I allowed to pass through my brain. (*Remember to cross through it.*)

_____

_____

_____

_____

_____

_____

_____

I spoke / invested this into myself today.

_____

_____

_____

_____

_____

_____

_____

_____

_____

_____

_____

_____

_____

_____

_____

_____

_____

_____

Week Three – Day Sixteen

Day: _____; Date: ____/____/____; Time: _____

Wrestle

"... And, behold, Jehovah passed by, and a great and strong wind rent the mountains, and brake in pieces the rocks before Jehovah; but Jehovah was not in the wind: and after the wind an earthquake; but Jehovah was not in the earthquake: and after the earthquake a fire; but Jehovah was not in the fire: and after the fire a still small voice."

1 Kings 19: 11, 12

My thought/ My Daydream

_____
_____
_____
_____
_____
_____

Today I daydreamed for _____ minutes.

A thought that I allowed to pass through my brain. (*Remember to cross through it.*)

_____

_____

_____

_____

_____

_____

I spoke / invested this into myself today.

_____

_____

_____

_____

_____

_____

_____

_____

_____

_____

_____

_____

_____

Week Three – Day Seventeen

Day: _____; Date: ____/____/____; Time: _____

Wrestle

*"I know how to be abased, and I know also how
to abound: in everything and in all things have
I learned the secret both to be filled and to be
hungry, both to abound and to be in want. I can
do all things in him that strengtheneth me."*

Philippians 4: 12, 13

My thought/ My Daydream

_____
_____
_____
_____
_____
_____

Today I daydreamed for _____ minutes.

A thought that I allowed to pass through my brain. (*Remember to cross through it.*)

_____

_____

_____

_____

_____

_____

I spoke / invested this into myself today.

_____

_____

_____

_____

_____

_____

_____

_____

_____

_____

_____

_____

_____

_____

_____

Week Three – Day Eighteen

Day: _____; Date: ____/____/____; Time: _____

Wrestle

"But ye, brethren, be not weary in well-doing."

2 Thessalonians 3: 13

My thought/ My Daydream

_____

_____

_____

_____

_____

_____

Today I daydreamed for _____ minutes.

A thought that I allowed to pass through my brain. (*Remember to cross through it.*)

I spoke / invested this into myself today.

Day: _____; Date: ____/____/____; Time: _____

Wrestle

"Ye are of God, little children, and have
overcome them: because greater is he that
is in you, than he that is in the world."

1 John 4: 4

My thought/ My Daydream

_____

_____

_____

_____

_____

_____

Today I daydreamed for _____ minutes.

A thought that I allowed to pass through my brain. (*Remember to cross through it.*)

_____

_____

_____

_____

_____

_____

I spoke / invested this into myself today.

_____

_____

_____

_____

_____

_____

_____

_____

_____

_____

_____

_____

_____

_____

Day: _____; Date: ____/____/____; Time: _____

Wrestle

"For God hath not given us the spirit of fear; but
of power, and of love, and of a sound mind."

2 Timothy 1: 7

My thought/ My Daydream

_____

_____

_____

_____

_____

_____

Today I daydreamed for _____ minutes.

A thought that I allowed to pass through my brain. (*Remember to cross through it.*)

_____

_____

_____

_____

_____

_____

I spoke / invested this into myself today.

_____

_____

_____

_____

_____

_____

_____

_____

_____

_____

_____

_____

_____

_____

_____

_____

Week Three – Day Twenty-one

Day: _____; Date: ____/____/____; Time: _____

Wrestle

"Finally, brethren, whatsoever things are honest, whatsoever things are just, whatsoever things are pure, whatsoever things are lovely, whatsoever things are of good report; if there be any virtue, and if there be any praise, think on these things."

Philippians 4: 8

My thought/ My Daydream

_____

_____

_____

_____

_____

_____

Today I daydreamed for _____ minutes.

A thought that I allowed to pass through my brain. (*Remember to cross through it.*)

_____

_____

_____

_____

_____

_____

_____

I spoke / invested this into myself today.

_____

_____

_____

_____

_____

_____

_____

_____

_____

_____

_____

_____

_____

_____

_____

_____

_____

Week Four

The week of ___/___/___ through ___/___/___

Your Weekly Motivation

*"For he that will love life, and see good
days, let him refrain his tongue from evil,
and his lips that they speak no guile:"*

1 Peter 3: 10

Word for the week – *Speak*
(Say something in order to convey information, an opinion, or a feeling.)

Maya Angelou was a great poet, author, and speaker. She used words to express with deep compassion the conditions of life. She knew the importance of words. She learned at a very young age that words can destroy and words can lift. She said, "I am convinced that words are things and we must be careful about the words we use or use in our homes. They get on the walls. They get into your wallpaper, they get in your upholstery, in your clothes, and finally into you."

Ralph Waldo Emerson said that words would become actions.

When we first see God in Genesis, we find Him creating through speaking. He is showing us the power of words. He spoke and the Holy Spirit moved.

Neuroscience says our brains are not designed to hold on to negative thoughts. It actually causes brain damage.

Our brains are designed to be controlled by the Holy Spirit. We must think positive thoughts, speak them and allow Holy Spirit to move in us and through us to accomplish our expected end.

Permit your positive thoughts which had their origin in the word of God, to become the words that you speak that causes the Holy Ghost to move catapulting you in the direction of destiny. ***Speak over yourself!!!***

Week Four – Day Twenty-two

Day: _____; Date: ____/____/____; Time: _____

Speak

*"Let the words of my mouth, and the meditation
of my heart, be acceptable in thy sight, O
LORD, my strength, and my redeemer."*

Psalm 19: 14

My thought/ My Daydream

_____

_____

_____

_____

_____

_____

Today I daydreamed for _____ minutes.

A thought that I allowed to pass through my brain. (*Remember to cross through it.*)

_____
_____
_____
_____
_____
_____
_____

I spoke / invested this into myself today.

_____
_____
_____
_____
_____
_____
_____
_____
_____
_____
_____
_____
_____
_____
_____
_____

Week Four – Day Twenty-three

Day: _____; Date: ____/____/____; Time: _____

Speak

"Death and life are in the power of the tongue:
and they that love it shall eat the fruit thereof."

Proverbs 18: 21

My thought/ My Daydream

_____
_____
_____
_____
_____
_____

Today I daydreamed for _____ minutes.

A thought that I allowed to pass through my brain. (*Remember to cross through it.*)

_____

_____

_____

_____

_____

_____

_____

I spoke / invested this into myself today.

_____

_____

_____

_____

_____

_____

_____

_____

_____

_____

_____

_____

_____

_____

_____

_____

_____

Week Four – Day Twenty-four

Day: _____; Date: ___/___/___; Time: _____

Speak

"Keep thy tongue from evil, and thy
lips from speaking guile."

Psalm 34: 13

My thought/ My Daydream

_____

_____

_____

_____

_____

_____

Today I daydreamed for _____ minutes.

A thought that I allowed to pass through my brain. (*Remember to cross through it.*)

_____

_____

_____

_____

_____

_____

I spoke / invested this into myself today.

_____

_____

_____

_____

_____

_____

_____

_____

_____

_____

_____

_____

_____

_____

_____

_____

Week Four – Day Twenty- five

Day: _____; Date: ____/____/____; Time: _____

Speak

"Set a watch, O LORD, before my
mouth; keep the door of my lips."

Psalm 141: 3

My thought/ My Daydream

_____

_____

_____

_____

_____

_____

Today I daydreamed for _____ minutes.

A thought that I allowed to pass through my brain. *(Remember to cross through it.)*

_____

_____

_____

_____

_____

_____

_____

I spoke / invested this into myself today.

_____

_____

_____

_____

_____

_____

_____

_____

_____

_____

_____

_____

_____

_____

_____

_____

_____

_____

Week Four – Day Twenty-six

Day: _____; Date: ____/____/____; Time: _____

Speak

"Keep thy heart with all diligence; for
out of it are the issues of life."

Proverbs 4: 23

My thought/ My Daydream

_____

_____

_____

_____

_____

_____

Today I daydreamed for _____ minutes.

A thought that I allowed to pass through my brain. (*Remember to cross through it.*)

_____

_____

_____

_____

_____

_____

_____

I spoke / invested this into myself today.

_____

_____

_____

_____

_____

_____

_____

_____

_____

_____

_____

_____

_____

_____

_____

_____

_____

Week Four – Day Twenty-seven

Day: _____; Date: ____/____/____; Time: _____

Speak

"The tongue of the wise useth knowledge aright:
but the mouth of fools poureth out foolishness."

Proverbs 15: 2

My thought/ My Daydream

_____
_____
_____
_____
_____
_____

Today I daydreamed for _____ minutes.

A thought that I allowed to pass through my brain. (*Remember to cross through it.*)

_____
_____
_____
_____
_____
_____
_____

I spoke / invested this into myself today.

_____
_____
_____
_____
_____
_____
_____
_____
_____
_____
_____
_____
_____
_____
_____
_____

Week Four – Day Twenty- eight

Day: _____; Date: ____/____/____; Time: _____

Speak

"Who is a wise man and endued with knowledge among you? Let him shew out of a good conversation his works with meekness of wisdom."

James 3: 13

My thought/ My Daydream

_____

_____

_____

_____

_____

_____

Today I daydreamed for _____ minutes.

A thought that I allowed to pass through my brain. (*Remember to cross through it.*)

_____
_____
_____
_____
_____
_____
_____

I spoke / invested this into myself today.

_____
_____
_____
_____
_____
_____
_____
_____
_____
_____
_____
_____
_____
_____
_____

Week Five

FORGIVE

WEEK FIVE: *FORGIVE*

The week of ___/___/___ through ___/___/___

Your Weekly Motivation

*"He hath not dealt with us after our sins; nor
rewarded us according to our iniquities. For
as the heaven is high above the earth, so great
is his mercy toward them that fear him."*

Psalms 103: 10, 11

Word for the week – *Forgive*

(Stop feeling angry or resentful toward [someone]
for an offense, flaw, or mistake.)

"Having resentment against someone is like drinking poison and expecting it to kill someone else." Nelson Mandela

Recently, I read the book, *Unforgiveness: The Antibacterial Angel by* Apostle Lee Christopher Roberson. While reading about the importance of forgiving others as well as myself, my thoughts went back to second grade. This is where my struggle with my deep-rooted feelings of being unattractive began. I did not realize that these feelings were restraining me; opportunities not pursued and acceptance of situations/ill treatments.

I had to forgive myself for things that I had done and for allowing certain people to repeatedly treat me in a particular way that was harmful to my psyche. I was great at forgiving others, but not myself. When I forgave myself, surprisingly, the feeling of being unattractive finally rose to the surface and I was able to deal with the root cause. But this change had to take place overtime. Who would have ever thought that my self- unforgiveness was allowing me to hold onto negative thoughts/opinions of myself?

When I dealt with it, my whole outlook on life changed. I am no longer bound by the fear of being rejected because I do not look like what I perceived as acceptable. I am who God says I am.

God has not given me a spirit of fear but of peace, love, and a sound mind. That spirit of fear was learned over time, it had to be unlearned. It did not come from God and I do not have to receive it or accept it.

Revisit the autobiography you wrote in the introduction section at the beginning of this journal. Examine it to see if there is a need for forgiveness. Unforgiveness is a form of self-abuse. With each feeling, we are constantly beating up on ourselves with no consequential productive manifestation.

We are created in the image of God; therefore, we are not designed to hold on to unforgiveness. ***Remember this: there will be no unforgiveness in Heaven!!!***

Day: _____; Date: ____/____/____; Time: _____

Forgive

*"And when ye stand praying, forgive, if ye have
ought against any: that your Father also which
is in heaven may forgive you your trespasses.
But if ye do not forgive, neither will your Father
which is in heaven forgive your trespasses."*

Mark 11: 25, 26

My thought/ My Daydream

_____
_____
_____
_____
_____
_____

Today I daydreamed for _____ minutes.

A thought that I allowed to pass through my brain. (*Remember to cross through it.*)

_____
_____
_____
_____
_____
_____

I spoke / invested this into myself today.

_____
_____
_____
_____
_____
_____
_____
_____
_____
_____
_____
_____
_____
_____

Week Five – Day Thirty

Day: _____; Date: ____/____/____; Time: _____

Forgive

"Then came Peter to him, and said, Lord, how oft shall my brother sin against me, and I forgive him? Till seven times? Jesus saith unto him, I say not unto thee, until seven times: but, until seventy times seven."

Matthew 18: 21, 22

My thought/ My Daydream

_____

_____

_____

_____

_____

_____

Today I daydreamed for _____ minutes.

A thought that I allowed to pass through my brain. (*Remember to cross through it.*)

_____

_____

_____

_____

_____

_____

_____

I spoke / invested this into myself today.

_____

_____

_____

_____

_____

_____

_____

_____

_____

_____

_____

_____

_____

_____

_____

_____

_____

Week Four – Day Thirty-one

Day: _____; Date: ____/____/____; Time: _____

Forgive

"And be ye kind one to another, tenderhearted,
forgiving one another, even as God for
Christ's sake hath forgiven you."

Ephesians 4: 32

My thought/ My Daydream

_____
_____
_____
_____
_____
_____

Today I daydreamed for _____ minutes.

A thought that I allowed to pass through my brain. (*Remember to cross through it.*)

_____

_____

_____

_____

_____

_____

_____

I spoke / invested this into myself today.

_____

_____

_____

_____

_____

_____

_____

_____

_____

_____

_____

_____

_____

_____

_____

_____

Week Five – Day Thirty-two

Day: _____; Date: ____/____/____; Time: _____

Forgive

"For thou, Lord, art good, and ready to forgive; and plenteous in mercy unto all them that call upon thee."

Psalm 86: 5

My thought/ My Daydream

_____

_____

_____

_____

_____

_____

Today I daydreamed for _____ minutes.

A thought that I allowed to pass through my brain. (*Remember to cross through it.*)

_____

_____

_____

_____

_____

_____

I spoke / invested this into myself today.

_____

_____

_____

_____

_____

_____

_____

_____

_____

_____

_____

_____

_____

_____

_____

Week Five – Day Thirty-three

Day: _____; Date: ____/____/____; Time: _____

Forgive

"If we confess our sins, he is faithful and just to forgive us our sins, and to cleanse us from all unrighteousness."

1 John 1: 9

My thought/ My Daydream

_____

_____

_____

_____

_____

_____

Today I daydreamed for _____ minutes.

A thought that I allowed to pass through my brain. (*Remember to cross through it.*)

_____

_____

_____

_____

_____

_____

_____

I spoke / invested this into myself today.

_____

_____

_____

_____

_____

_____

_____

_____

_____

_____

_____

_____

_____

_____

_____

_____

Week Five – Day Thirty-four

Day: _____ ; Date: ____/____/____ ; Time: _____

Forgive

*"Therefore if any man be in Christ, he is a
new creature: old things are passed away;
behold, all things are become new."*

2 Corinthians 5: 17

My thought/ My Daydream

_____
_____
_____
_____
_____
_____

Today I daydreamed for _____ minutes.

A thought that I allowed to pass through my brain. (*Remember to cross through it.*)

_____

_____

_____

_____

_____

_____

_____

I spoke / invested this into myself today.

_____

_____

_____

_____

_____

_____

_____

_____

_____

_____

_____

_____

_____

_____

_____

_____

_____

Week Five – Day Thirty-five

Day: _____ ; Date: ____/____/____ ; Time: _____

Forgive

*"There is therefore now no condemnation
to them which are in Christ Jesus, who walk
not after the flesh, but after the Spirit."*

Romans 8: 1

My thought/ My Daydream

_____
_____
_____
_____
_____
_____

Today I daydreamed for _____ minutes.

A thought that I allowed to pass through my brain. (*Remember to cross through it.*)

_____

_____

_____

_____

_____

_____

_____

I spoke / invested this into myself today.

_____

_____

_____

_____

_____

_____

_____

_____

_____

_____

_____

_____

_____

_____

_____

_____

Week Six

Addicted.

WEEK SIX: *ADDICTED TO GOD*

The week of ___/___/___ through ___/___/___

Your Weekly Motivation

"And God said, Let us make man in our image, after our likeness:..."

Genesis 1: 26

Word for the week – *Addicted*

(Physical and mentally dependent on a particular substance, and unable to stop taking it without incurring adverse effects; enthusiastically devoted to a particular thing or activity.)

In the first chapter of Genesis verse 11, God called forth the grass, herbs, and trees out of the earth and that is where they must stay to survive. In the soil are all the essentials for the plants to grow and become the grass, herbs and trees God called them to be; roots, stems, and leaves just for its terrestrial habitat. The soil even had the provisions for the future seeds to go from germination to maturity.

In verse 21, God said let the waters bring forth abundantly the moving creatures that hath life and in the water they must stay in order to survive. The water, like the soil, had all the provisions for the moving creatures. The creatures had all the adaptations needed to be able to move and acquire substance for survival; fins, flippers and gills just for its aquatic environment and none other.

In verses 26 and 27, *"God said let us make man in our image, after our likeness... So God created man in his own image, the image of God created He him; male and female created He them."* Genesis 2: 7, *"And the LORD God formed man of the dust of the ground, and breathed into his nostrils the breath of life; and man became a living soul."* We came out of God and we cannot live without Him. He has given us a mind, body, and soul so that we may stay in relationship with Him. The quality and quantity of our lives is contingent upon this relationship. It is in Him that we move, live, and have our being. We are ADDICTED to Him.[4] When we act contrary to Him, our source of life, we are slowly dying. We lose our sense of self-worth and all our accomplishments seem worthless.

Speaking negative words incompatible to our relational environment have adverse effects in the human body. Our minds are designed to go where our thoughts go.[5] Keep in mind that He endured the cross just so we can sustain a life favorable to receive an eternal existence.

This week analyze your negative thoughts, learn from them and keep moving in the direction of greater. Stay in relationship with God and LIVE!!!

Week Six – Day Thirty-six

Day: _____; Date: ____/____/____; Time: _____

Addicted

"For we are his workmanship, created in Christ Jesus unto good works, which God hath before ordained that we should walk in them."

Ephesians 2: 10

My thought/ My Daydream

_____
_____
_____
_____
_____
_____

Today I daydreamed for _____ minutes.

A thought that I allowed to pass through my brain. (*Remember to cross through it.*)

_____
_____
_____
_____
_____
_____
_____

I spoke / invested this into myself today.

_____
_____
_____
_____
_____
_____
_____
_____
_____
_____
_____
_____
_____
_____
_____
_____
_____

Week Six – Day Thirty-seven

Day: _____; Date: ____/____/____; Time: _____

Addicted

"For in Him we live, and move, and have our being; as certain also of your own poets have said, For we are also his offspring."

Acts 17: 28

My thought/ My Daydream

_____

_____

_____

_____

_____

_____

Today I daydreamed for _____ minutes.

A thought that I allowed to pass through my brain. (*Remember to cross through it.*)

_____
_____
_____
_____
_____
_____
_____

I spoke / invested this into myself today.

_____
_____
_____
_____
_____
_____
_____
_____
_____
_____
_____
_____
_____
_____
_____
_____

Week Six – Day Thirty-eight

Day: _____; Date: ____/____/____; Time: _____

Addicted

"But ye are not in the flesh, but in the Spirit, if so be that the Spirit of God dwell in you. Now if any man has not the Spirit of Chris, he is none of his."

Romans 8: 9

My thought/ My Daydream

_____
_____
_____
_____
_____
_____

Today I daydreamed for _____ minutes.

A thought that I allowed to pass through my brain. (*Remember to cross through it.*)

_____
_____
_____
_____
_____
_____
_____

I spoke / invested this into myself today.

_____
_____
_____
_____
_____
_____
_____
_____
_____
_____
_____
_____
_____
_____
_____
_____
_____

Week Six – Day Thirty-nine

Day: _____; Date: ___/___/___; Time: _____

Addicted

"And ye are Christ's; and Christ is God's."

1 Corinthians 3: 23

My thought/ My Daydream

_____
_____
_____
_____
_____
_____

Today I daydreamed for _____ minutes.

A thought that I allowed to pass through my brain. (*Remember to cross through it.*)

_____
_____
_____
_____
_____
_____
_____

I spoke / invested this into myself today.

_____
_____
_____
_____
_____
_____
_____
_____
_____
_____
_____
_____
_____
_____
_____
_____
_____
_____

Week Six – Day Forty

Day: _____; Date: ____/____/____; Time: _____

Addicted

"For ye are bought with a price: therefore glorify God in your body, and in your spirit, which are God's."

1 Corinthians 6: 20

My thought/ My Daydream

_____

_____

_____

_____

_____

_____

Today I daydreamed for _____ minutes.

A thought that I allowed to pass through my brain. (*Remember to cross through it.*)

_____
_____
_____
_____
_____
_____
_____

I spoke / invested this into myself today.

_____
_____
_____
_____
_____
_____
_____
_____
_____
_____
_____
_____
_____
_____
_____
_____
_____
_____

Week Six – Day Forty-one

Day: _____; Date: ____/____/____; Time: _____

Addicted

"I am the vine, ye are the branches: He that abideth
in me, and I in him, the same bringeth forth much
fruit: for without me ye can do nothing."

John 15: 5

My thought/ My Daydream

_____

_____

_____

_____

_____

_____

Today I daydreamed for _____ minutes.

A thought that I allowed to pass through my brain. (*Remember to cross through it.*)

_____

_____

_____

_____

_____

_____

_____

I spoke / invested this into myself today.

_____

_____

_____

_____

_____

_____

_____

_____

_____

_____

_____

_____

_____

_____

_____

_____

_____

Week Six – Day Forty-two

Day: _____; Date: ____/____/____; Time: _____

Addicted

*"I will praise thee; for I am fearfully and
wonderfully made: marvelous are thy works;
and that my soul knoweth right well."*

Psalm 139: 14

My thought/ My Daydream

_____
_____
_____
_____
_____
_____

Today I daydreamed for _____ minutes.

A thought that I allowed to pass through my brain. *(Remember to cross through it.)*

_____

_____

_____

_____

_____

_____

I spoke / invested this into myself today.

_____

_____

_____

_____

_____

_____

_____

_____

_____

_____

_____

_____

_____

_____

Week Seven

WEEK SEVEN: *POTENTIAL*

The week of ___/___/___ through ___/___/___

"So God created man in his own image, in the image of God created he him; male and female created he them."

Genesis 1: 27

Word for the week – *Potential*

(Having or showing the capacity to become or develop into something in the future; latent qualities or abilities that may be developed and lead to future success or usefulness.)

My Pastor, Bishop Michael A. Blue said to me, actually it was in a sermon, but I took it personal, "You are not the you, YOU will become." These words changed my whole perspective of life. Just to know it will not be this way always, stirred up my inner self. I realized that all I needed was to just keep living and I would walk into greater. For the scripture proclaims, my latter will be greater. Each day is a latter for the previous and present day. If with each day there is a greater, then there is no end in my potential. If I can think it or do it, God can take me beyond it.

Be encouraged in knowing that you come from an all-knowing and all-powerful God. There is no end or boundaries to confine Him.

We often encourage the youth by referring to the

potential they have within. As adults, we too have potential and it does not end with retirement or old age.

A few years ago, Bishop T.D. Jakes had an interview with my pastor. In the interview, my pastor asked him did he know he had all that in him; musician, pastor, speaker, author, business owner, and movie producer. His response really blessed me. He took us to Malachi 3: 10, *"Bring ye all the tithes into the storehouse, that there may be meat in mine house, and prove me now herewith, saith the LORD of hosts, if I will not open you the windows of heaven, and pour you out a blessing, that there shall not be room enough to receive it."* He explained that there is one blessing and many windows. His blessing was the gift of communication and the others, the windows; were all forms of communication. God gave him one blessing and all the other gifts he implements are windows. Some gifts do have a shelf-life as to how they are expressed. I taught school for a little more than forty years. Since retiring from the classroom, I do not get to stand before students, but I am still expressing my gift of teaching through writing; same gift, another window. If we determine what our blessing is, then, we can see the potential windows and not be afraid to walk into an array of possibilities. What is your one blessing?!!!

This week give a great amount of thought through

prayer as to what is your blessing. The songwriter wrote, "We need a blessing, a blessing from you. Just one blessing will do. ..." When this is taken in context of windows, a blessing will do, for it has many avenues; great *potential*.

Week Seven – Day Forty-three

Day: _____; Date: ____/____/____; Time: _____

Potential

"But Jesus beheld them, and said unto them, With men this is impossible; but with God all things are possible."

Matthew 19: 26

My thought/ My Daydream

_____

_____

_____

_____

_____

_____

Today I daydreamed for _____ minutes.

A thought that I allowed to pass through my brain. (*Remember to cross through it.*)

_____

_____

_____

_____

_____

_____

I spoke / invested this into myself today.

_____

_____

_____

_____

_____

_____

_____

_____

_____

_____

_____

_____

_____

_____

_____

Day: _____; Date: ____/____/____; Time: _____

Potential

*"Therefore I say unto you, What things
soever ye desire, when ye pray, believe that ye
receive them, and ye shall have them."*

Mark 11: 24

My thought/ My Daydream

_____

_____

_____

_____

_____

_____

Today I daydreamed for _____ minutes.

A thought that I allowed to pass through my brain. (*Remember to cross through it.*)

_____
_____
_____
_____
_____
_____

I spoke / invested this into myself today.

_____
_____
_____
_____
_____
_____
_____
_____
_____
_____
_____
_____
_____
_____
_____

Week Seven – Day Forty-five

Day: _____; Date: ____/____/____; Time: _____

Potential

"But we see Jesus, who was made a little lower than the angels for the suffering of death, crowned with glory and honour; that he by the grace of God should taste death for every man."

Hebrews 2: 9

My thought/ My Daydream

_____

_____

_____

_____

_____

_____

Today I daydreamed for _____ minutes.

A thought that I allowed to pass through my brain. (*Remember to cross through it.*)

_____
_____
_____
_____
_____
_____

I spoke / invested this into myself today.

_____
_____
_____
_____
_____
_____
_____
_____
_____
_____
_____
_____
_____
_____
_____
_____

Week Seven – Day Forty-six

Day: _____; Date: ____/____/____; Time: _____

Potential

"Now unto him that is able to do exceeding
abundantly above all that we ask or think,
according to the power that worketh in us, ..."

Ephesians 3: 20

My thought/ My Daydream

_____

_____

_____

_____

_____

_____

Today I daydreamed for _____ minutes.

A thought that I allowed to pass through my brain. (*Remember to cross through it.*)

_____

_____

_____

_____

_____

_____

_____

I spoke / invested this into myself today.

_____

_____

_____

_____

_____

_____

_____

_____

_____

_____

_____

_____

_____

_____

_____

_____

_____

Week Seven – Day Forty-seven

Day: _____; Date: ____/____/____; Time: _____

Potential

"I can do all things through Christ
which strengtheneth me."

Philippians 4: 13

My thought/ My Daydream

_____

_____

_____

_____

_____

_____

Today I daydreamed for _____ minutes.

A thought that I allowed to pass through my brain. (*Remember to cross through it.*)

_____

_____

_____

_____

_____

_____

_____

I spoke / invested this into myself today.

_____

_____

_____

_____

_____

_____

_____

_____

_____

_____

_____

_____

_____

_____

_____

Week Seven – Day Forty-eight

Day: _____; Date: ____/____/____; Time: _____

Potential

"Meditate upon these things; give thyself wholly
to them; that thy profiting may appear to all."

1Timothy 4: 15

My thought/ My Daydream

_____

_____

_____

_____

_____

_____

Today I daydreamed for _____ minutes.

A thought that I allowed to pass through my brain. (*Remember to cross through it.*)

_____

_____

_____

_____

_____

_____

I spoke / invested this into myself today.

_____

_____

_____

_____

_____

_____

_____

_____

_____

_____

_____

_____

_____

_____

_____

Week Seven – Day Forty-nine

Day: _____; Date: ____/____/____; Time: _____

Potential

*"And now, brethren, I commend you to God,
and to the word of his grace, which is able to
build you up, and to give you an inheritance
among all them which are sanctified."*

Acts 20: 32

My thought/ My Daydream

_____

_____

_____

_____

_____

_____

Today I daydreamed for _____ minutes.

A thought that I allowed to pass through my brain. (*Remember to cross through it.*)

_____

_____

_____

_____

_____

_____

_____

I spoke / invested this into myself today.

_____

_____

_____

_____

_____

_____

_____

_____

_____

_____

_____

_____

_____

_____

_____

_____

_____

Week Eight

PLEASURE

WEEK EIGHT: *GOD'S PLEASURE*

The week of ___/___/___ through ___/___/___

"Fear not, little flock; for it is your Father's good pleasure to give you the kingdom."

Luke 12: 32

Word for the week – *Pleasure*

(A feeling of happy satisfaction and enjoyment.)

This week is to emphasize God's love for you and towards you. It is to show that you are important to Him and He takes pleasure in blessing you. God loves all. John 3: 16 says, *"For God so loved the world, that he gave his only begotten Son, that whosoever believeth in him should not perish, but have everlasting life."*

He takes special pleasure in those that honor Him and obey His commandments. The late Bishop Dr. Charles O. McDowell said of his girls, "I, like all parents, love all my children, but when one is consistently obedient, just a good child, I look for something to give her… just because." He went further to say, "That's how God feels about us when we line up our lives according to His will."

There is pleasure in His giving. Read **Deuteronomy 28.**

His giving is not only tangible, He says in Isaiah 43:4, *"Since thou wast precious in my sight, thou hast been honourable, and I have loved thee: Therefore, will I give men for thee, and people for thy life."* Take a look around you. There are people in your life that have loved, helped, and pushed you. They are all gifts from God to help usher you into your destiny.

In primary school we sang:

Jesus loves the little children.
All the little children of the world;
Red, yellow, black, and white,
They are all precious in His sight.
Jesus loves the little children of the world.

George Frederick Root

Are you not His child, precious in His sight?!

Week Eight – Day Fifty

Day: _____; Date: ____/____/____; Time: _____

Pleasure

"Thou art worthy, O Lord, to receive glory and honour and power: for thou hast created all things, and for thy pleasure they are and were created."

Revelation 4: 11

My thought/ My Daydream

_____

_____

_____

_____

_____

_____

Today I daydreamed for _____ minutes.

A thought that I allowed to pass through my brain. (*Remember to cross through it.*)

_____

_____

_____

_____

_____

_____

I spoke / invested this into myself today.

_____

_____

_____

_____

_____

_____

_____

_____

_____

_____

_____

_____

_____

_____

Week Eight – Day Fifty-one

Day: _____; Date: ____/____/____; Time: _____

Pleasure

"Since thou wast precious in my sight, thou hast been honourable, and I have loved thee: Therefore will I give men for thee, and people for thy life."

Isaiah 43: 4

My thought/ My Daydream

_____

_____

_____

_____

_____

_____

Today I daydreamed for _____ minutes.

A thought that I allowed to pass through my brain. *(Remember to cross through it.)*

_____

_____

_____

_____

_____

_____

I spoke / invested this into myself today.

_____

_____

_____

_____

_____

_____

_____

_____

_____

_____

_____

_____

_____

_____

_____

Week Eight – Day Fifty-two

Day: _____; Date: ____/____/____; Time: _____

Pleasure

"Even everyone that is called by my name:
for I have created him for my glory, I have
formed him; yea, I have made him."

Isaiah 43: 7

My thought/ My Daydream

_____
_____
_____
_____
_____
_____

Today I daydreamed for _____ minutes.

A thought that I allowed to pass through my brain. *(Remember to cross through it.)*

_____

_____

_____

_____

_____

_____

_____

I spoke / invested this into myself today.

_____

_____

_____

_____

_____

_____

_____

_____

_____

_____

_____

_____

_____

_____

_____

_____

Week Eight – Day Fifty-three

Day: _____; Date: ____/____/____; Time: _____

Pleasure

"But God commendeth his love toward us, in that while we were yet sinners, Christ died for us."

Romans 5: 8

My thought/ My Daydream

_____

_____

_____

_____

_____

_____

Today I daydreamed for _____ minutes.

A thought that I allowed to pass through my brain. (*Remember to cross through it.*)

_____

_____

_____

_____

_____

_____

I spoke / invested this into myself today.

_____

_____

_____

_____

_____

_____

_____

_____

_____

_____

_____

_____

_____

_____

_____

_____

Week Eight – Day Fifty-four

Day: _____; Date: ____/____/____; Time: _____

Pleasure

"The steps of a good man are ordered by the LORD: and he delighteth in his way."

Psalm 37: 23

My thought/ My Daydream

_____

_____

_____

_____

_____

_____

Today I daydreamed for _____ minutes.

A thought that I allowed to pass through my brain. (*Remember to cross through it.*)

_____

_____

_____

_____

_____

_____

_____

I spoke / invested this into myself today.

_____

_____

_____

_____

_____

_____

_____

_____

_____

_____

_____

_____

_____

_____

_____

_____

_____

Week Eight – Day Fifty-five

Day: _____; Date: ____/____/____; Time: _____

Pleasure

"For the LORD taketh pleasure in his people:
he will beautify the meek with salvation."

Psalm 149: 4

My thought/ My Daydream

_____

_____

_____

_____

_____

_____

Today I daydreamed for _____ minutes.

A thought that I allowed to pass through my brain. (*Remember to cross through it.*)

_____

_____

_____

_____

_____

_____

I spoke / invested this into myself today.

_____

_____

_____

_____

_____

_____

_____

_____

_____

_____

_____

_____

_____

_____

Week Eight – Day Fifty-six

Day: _____; Date: ____/____/____; Time: _____

Pleasure

"Delight thyself also in the LORD; and he shall give thee the desires of thine heart."

Psalm 37: 4

My thought/ My Daydream

_____

_____

_____

_____

_____

_____

Today I daydreamed for _____ minutes.

A thought that I allowed to pass through my brain. (*Remember to cross through it.*)

_____
_____
_____
_____
_____
_____
_____

I spoke / invested this into myself today.

_____
_____
_____
_____
_____
_____
_____
_____
_____
_____
_____
_____
_____
_____
_____
_____

Week Nine

WEEK NINE: *MORE*

The week of ___/___/___ through ___/___/___

"Therefore leaving the principles of the doctrine of Christ, let us go on unto perfection; not laying again the foundation of repentance from dead works, and of faith toward God,..."

Hebrews 6: 1

Word for the week – *More*

(Comparative of many, much; greater or additional amount or degree.)

You are nearing the end of your 63 day journey. It is my prayer that you have acquired a taste for "MORE". You want to do more of cleaning up defeating thoughts and speaking more productively.

Take time this final week to review the previous motivational topics. Maintain your high by stimulating the release of neurotransmitters that keep you encouraged. Pursue, go after the positive things in life. Wrestle with God until there is a life change. Always speak positive and forgive yourself for accepting and holding on to self-defeating thoughts or actions. You are an addict, addicted to the One that is Omnipotent; you cannot live without Him. There is an unlimited amount of potential in you, so keep it moving. He is love and finds great pleasure in blessing those that love Him and keep His commandments.

There is a greater plan that God has for you. Your thoughts are steering you to an expected end. As your thoughts and words become more intentional, you become joyful, relaxed, and more self-acceptable.

I pray you are inspired to seek, desire, and want more of Him. It is through the knowledge of Him that we become more like Him, the way we were designed.

Week Nine – Day Fifty-seven

Day: _____; Date: ____/____/____; Time: _____

More

"But my God shall supply all your need according
to his riches in glory by Christ Jesus."

Philippians 4: 19

My thought/ My Daydream

_____

_____

_____

_____

_____

_____

Today I daydreamed for _____ minutes.

A thought that I allowed to pass through my brain. (*Remember to cross through it.*)

_____

_____

_____

_____

_____

_____

I spoke / invested this into myself today.

_____

_____

_____

_____

_____

_____

_____

_____

_____

_____

_____

_____

_____

_____

_____

_____

Week Nine – Day Fifty-eight

Day: _____; Date: ____/____/____; Time: _____

More

"A good man out of the treasure of his heart
bringeth forth that which is good: ...."

Luke 6: 45

My thought/ My Daydream

_____
_____
_____
_____
_____
_____

Today I daydreamed for _____ minutes.

A thought that I allowed to pass through my brain. *(Remember to cross through it.)*

_____

_____

_____

_____

_____

_____

I spoke / invested this into myself today.

_____

_____

_____

_____

_____

_____

_____

_____

_____

_____

_____

_____

_____

_____

_____

Week Nine – Day Fifty-nine

Day: _____; Date: ____/____/____; Time: _____

More

*"Trust in the LORD with all thine heart; and lean
not unto thine own understanding. In all thy ways
acknowledge him, and he shall direct thy paths."*

Proverbs 3: 5, 6

My thought/ My Daydream

_____

_____

_____

_____

_____

_____

Today I daydreamed for _____ minutes.

A thought that I allowed to pass through my brain. (*Remember to cross through it.*)

_____
_____
_____
_____
_____
_____
_____

I spoke / invested this into myself today.

_____
_____
_____
_____
_____
_____
_____
_____
_____
_____
_____
_____
_____
_____
_____
_____
_____

Day: _____; Date: ____/____/____; Time: _____

More

"Now the God of hope fill you with all joy and peace in believing, that ye may abound in hope, through the power of the Holy Ghost."

Romans 15: 13

My thought/ My Daydream

_____

_____

_____

_____

_____

_____

Today I daydreamed for _____ minutes.

A thought that I allowed to pass through my brain. (*Remember to cross through it.*)

_____

_____

_____

_____

_____

_____

I spoke / invested this into myself today.

_____

_____

_____

_____

_____

_____

_____

_____

_____

_____

_____

_____

_____

_____

_____

Week Nine – Day Sixty-one

Day: _____; Date: _____/_____/_____; Time: _____

More

"What shall we then say to these things? If
God be for us, who can be against us?"

Romans 8: 31

My thought/ My Daydream

_____

_____

_____

_____

_____

_____

Today I daydreamed for _____ minutes.

A thought that I allowed to pass through my brain. (*Remember to cross through it.*)

_____

_____

_____

_____

_____

_____

I spoke / invested this into myself today.

_____

_____

_____

_____

_____

_____

_____

_____

_____

_____

_____

_____

_____

_____

_____

_____

Week Nine – Day Sixty-two

Day: _____; Date: ____/____/____; Time: _____

More

*"As newborn babes, desire the sincere milk of
the word, that ye may grow thereby: if so be
ye have tasted that the Lord is gracious."*

1 Peter 2: 2, 3

My thought/ My Daydream

_____

_____

_____

_____

_____

_____

Today I daydreamed for _____ minutes.

A thought that I allowed to pass through my brain. (*Remember to cross through it.*)

_____
_____
_____
_____
_____
_____

I spoke / invested this into myself today.

_____
_____
_____
_____
_____
_____
_____
_____
_____
_____
_____
_____
_____
_____

Week Nine – Day Sixty-three

Day: _____; Date: ____/____/____; Time: _____

More

*"But grow in grace, and in the knowledge of
our Lord and Saviour Jesus Christ. To him
be glory both now and for ever. Amen."*

2 Peter 3 18

My thought/ My Daydream

_____
_____
_____
_____
_____
_____

Today I daydreamed for _____ minutes.

A thought that I allowed to pass through my brain. (*Remember to cross through it.*)

_____
_____
_____
_____
_____
_____

I spoke / invested this into myself today.

_____
_____
_____
_____
_____
_____
_____
_____
_____
_____
_____
_____
_____
_____
_____
_____
_____

Conclusion

You have now completed a nine week journey to change, through journaling your daydreams and positive thoughts. This process has been about creating a way of thinking that will allow you to perceive life as ***always favorable*** to you. Watch out for things that bring about or trigger a negative thought. Remember to immediately let it pass and replace it with positive thoughts and visions. Charles Stanley said, "Think what God thinks; the most powerful thoughts there are. God thoughts are the best thoughts." And keep yourself energized by maintaining a high!!!

Let's end with prayer.

Thank You God for this sister/brother. I pray that because of their dedication and determination to have a transformed mind and a transformed life, you will direct them to a path of destiny and show forth your loving-kindness. Thank you for what they have accomplished these 63 days and in days to come. Keep them encouraged! And if circumstances try to pull them back to negative thinking, guide their thoughts, their words, and their faith.

We thank You and bless You. AMEN

Art Credits

All drawings were done by the author.

Acknowledgements

Thank you **Patricia Crump McRae** for your dedication to the fulfillment of my dreams. I could not ask for a better friend.

Thank you **Sadarryle Evette Stephens**, my daughter, for taking this journey with me.

Thank you to all my **supporters**. Your positive inputs and prayers have been a constant source of strength and encouragement.

Bibliography

Biblical scriptures were taken from The King James version of the Bible.

All definitions are from the *New Oxford American Dictionary*. Internet.

My Dream/My Thoughts
[1] Leaf, Caroline. *"Planetshakers Conference: Part One."* Southbank, Victoria, Australia. August 14, 2019.

Daydream!!!
[2] Leaf, Caroline. *"Planetshakers Conference: Part One."* Southbank, Victoria, Australia. August 14, 2019.

WEEK ONE: **MAINTAIN YOUR HIGH**
[3] Leaf, Caroline. *"Planetshakers Conference: Part One."* Southbank, Victoria, Australia. August 14, 2019.

WEEK SIX: **ADDICTED TO GOD**
[4] Leaf, Caroline. *"Planetshakers Conference: Part One."* Southbank, Victoria, Australia August 14, 2019
[5] Ibid.

About the Author

Rachel is a wife, mother, grandmother, retired high school science educator, and an ordained minister. She holds a BS in Secondary Science Education, MAT in Biology, and a DMin. Her love for people has been expressed in teaching and in ministry. It is out of these experiences that she presents this journal. It is her belief that everyday presents opportunities to become better and if they are taken advantage of it will lead to change.

Printed in the United States
by Baker & Taylor Publisher Services